Ars Recte Vivendi
Being Essays Contributed To "The Easy Chair"

by

George William Curtis

Ars Recte Vivendi
Being Essays Contributed To "The Easy Chair"
by George William Curtis

ISBN: 978-93-59955-66-7

Published by

DOUBLE 9 BOOKS

2/13-B, Ansari Road
Daryaganj, New Delhi – 110002
info@double9books.com
www.double9books.com
Tel. 011-40042856

ABOUT THE AUTHOR

George William Curtis was an American author, reformer, public speaker, and political leader who was born on February 24, 1824, and died on August 31, 1892. He wanted to end slavery and fight for the rights of African Americans and Native Americans under the law. He also fought for women's right to vote, changes to the way the government works, and public schools. His birthday is February 24, 1824, and he was born in Providence, Rhode Island. The man who raised him was also named George Curtis. Mary Elizabeth (Burrill) Curtis, his mother, was the daughter of former U.S. Senator James Burrill Jr. She died when George was only two years old. Young George was sent to school in Jamaica Plain, Massachusetts, with his older brother James Burrill Curtis when he was six years old. He stayed there for five years. After his father got married again and was happy, the boys were brought back to Providence in 1835. They stayed there until around 1839, when they went to New York with their father. After three years, George and James connected with the transcendental movement's ideas and took part in the Brook Farm trial from 1842 to 1843. George lived close to Ralph Waldo Emerson for two years after leaving Brook Farm, in New York and Concord, Massachusetts.

CONTENTS

PREFACE

The publication of this collection of Essays was suggested by some remarks of a college professor, in the course of which he said that about a dozen of the "Easy Chair" Essays in Harper's Magazine so nearly cover the more vital questions of hygiene, courtesy, and morality that they might be gathered into a volume entitled "Ars Recte Vivendi," and as such they are offered to the public.

EXTRAVAGANCE AT COLLEGE

Young Sardanapalus recently remarked that the only trouble with his life in college was that the societies and clubs, the boating and balling, and music and acting, and social occupations of many kinds, left him no time for study. He had the best disposition to treat the faculty fairly, and to devote a proper attention to various branches of learning, and he was sincerely sorry that his other college engagements made it quite impossible. Before coming to college he thought that it might be practicable to mingle a little Latin and Greek, and possibly a touch of history and mathematics, with the more pressing duties of college life; but unless you could put more hours into the day, or more days into the week, he really did not see how it could be done.

It was the life of Sardanapalus in college which was the text of some sober speeches at Commencement dinners during the summer, and of many excellent articles in the newspapers. They all expressed a feeling which has been growing very rapidly and becoming very strong among old graduates, that college is now a very different place from the college which they remembered, and that young men now spend in a college year what young men in college formerly thought would be a very handsome sum for them to spend annually when they were established in the world. If any reader should chance to recall a little book of reminiscences by Dr. Tomes, which was published a few years ago, he will have a vivid picture of the life of forty and more years ago at a small New England college; and the similar records of other colleges at that time show how it was possible for a poor clergyman starving upon a meagre salary to send son after son to college. The collegian lived in a plain room, and upon very plain fare; he had no "extras," and the decorative expense of Sardanapalus was unknown. In the vacations he taught school or worked upon the farm. He knew that his father had paid by his own hard work for every dollar that he spent, and the relaxation of the sense of the duty of economy which always accompanies great riches had not yet begun. Sixty years ago the number of Americans who did not feel that they must live by their own labor was so small that it was not a class. But there is now a class of rich men's sons.

The average rate of living at college differs. One of the newspapers, in discussing the question, said that in most of the New England colleges a steady and sturdy young man need not spend more than six hundred dollars during the four years. This is obviously too low an estimate. Another thinks that the average rate at Harvard is probably from six hundred to ten hundred a year. Another computes a fair liberal average in the smaller New England colleges to be from twenty-four to twenty-six hundred dollars for the four years, and the last class at Williams is reported to have ranged from an average of six hundred and fifty dollars in the first year to seven hundred and twenty-eight dollars in the Senior. But the trouble lies in Sardanapalus. The mischief that he does is quite disproportioned to the number of him. In a class of one hundred the number of rich youth may be very small. But a college class is an American community in which every member is necessarily strongly affected by all social influences.

A few "fellows" living in princely extravagance in superbly furnished rooms, with every device of luxury, entertaining profusely, elected into all the desirable clubs and societies, conforming to another taste and another fashion than that of the college, form a class which is separate and exclusive, and which looks down on those who cannot enter the charmed circle. This is galling to the pride of the young man who cannot compete. The sense of the inequality is constantly refreshed. He may, indeed, attend closely to his studies. He may "scorn delights, and live laborious days." He may hug his threadbare coat and gloat over his unrugged floor as the fitting circumstance of "plain living and high thinking." It is always open to character and intellect to perceive and to assert their essential superiority. Why should Socrates heed Sardanapalus? Why indeed? But the average young man at college is not an ascetic, nor a devotee, nor an absorbed student unmindful of cold and heat, and disdainful of elegance and ease and the nameless magic of social accomplishment and grace. He is a youth peculiarly susceptible to the very influence that Sardanapalus typifies, and the wise parent will hesitate before sending his son to Sybaris rather than to Sparta.

When the presence of Sardanapalus at Harvard was criticised as dangerous and lamentable, the President promptly denied that the youth abounded at the university, or that his influence was wide-spread. He was there undoubtedly, and he sometimes misused his riches. But he had not established a standard, and he had not affected the life of the university, whose moral character could be favorably compared with that of any college. But even if the case were worse, it is not evident that a remedy is at hand. As the President suggested, there are two kinds of rich youth at college. There are the sons of those who have been always accustomed to riches, and who are generally neither vulgar nor extravagant, neither ostentatious nor profuse; and the sons of the "new rich," who are like men drunk with new wine, and who act accordingly.

The "new rich" parent will naturally send his son to Harvard, because it is the oldest of our colleges and of great renown, and because he supposes that through his college associations his son may pave a path with gold into "society." Harvard, on her part, opens her doors upon the same conditions to rich and poor, and gives her instruction equally, and requires only obedience to her rules of order and discipline. If Sardanapalus fails in his examination he will be dropped, and that he is Sardanapalus will not save him. If his revels disturb the college peace, he will be warned and dismissed. All that can be asked of the college is that it shall grant no grace to the golden youth in the hope of endowment from his father, and that it shall keep its own peace.

This last condition includes more than keeping technical order. To remove for cause in the civil service really means not only to remove for a penal offence, but for habits and methods that destroy discipline and efficiency. So to keep the peace in a college means to remove the necessary causes of disturbance and disorder. If young Sardanapalus, by his extravagance and riotous profusion and dissipation, constantly thwarts the essential purpose of the college, demoralizing the students and obstructing the peaceful course of its instruction, he ought to be dismissed. The college must judge the conditions under which its work may be most properly and efficiently accomplished, and to achieve its purpose it may justly limit the liberty of its students.

The solution of the difficulty lies more in the power of the students than of the college. If the young men who are the natural social leaders make simplicity the unwritten law of college social life, young Sardanapalus will spend his money and heap up luxury in vain. The simplicity and good sense of wealth will conquer its ostentation and reckless waste.

(*October*, 1886)

BRAINS AND BRAWN

It is towards the end of June and in the first days of July that the great college aquatic contests occur, and it is about that time, as the soldiers at Monmouth knew in 1778, that Sirius is lord of the ascendant. This year it was the hottest day of the summer, as marked by the mercury in New York, when the Harvard and Yale men drew out at New London for their race. Fifty years ago the crowd at Commencement filled the town green and streets, and the meeting-house in which the graduating class were the heroes of the hour. The valedictorian, the salutatorian, the philosophical orator, walked on air, and the halo of after-triumphs of many kinds was not brighter or more intoxicating than the brief glory of the moment on which they took the graduating stage, under the beaming eyes of maiden beauty and the profound admiration of college comrades.

Willis, as Phil Slingsby, has told the story of that college life fifty and sixty years ago. The collegian danced and drove and flirted and dined and sang the night away. Robert Tomes echoed the strain in his tale of college life a little later, under stricter social and ecclesiastical conditions. There was a more serious vein also. In 1827 the Kappa Alpha Society was the first of the younger brood of the Greek alphabet—descendants of the Phi Beta Kappa of 1781—and in 1832 Father Eells, as he is affectionately called, founded Alpha Delta Phi, a brotherhood based upon other aims and sympathies than those of Mr. Philip Slingsby, but one which appealed instantly to clever men in college, and has not ceased to attract them to this happy hour, as the Easy Chair has just now commemorated.

But neither in the sketches of Slingsby nor in the memories of those Commencement triumphs is there any record of an absorbing and universal and overpowering enthusiasm such as attends the modern college boat-race. The race of this year between the two great New England universities, Harvard and Yale—the Crimson and the Blue—was a twilight contest, for "high-water," says the careful chronicler, "did not occur until seven o'clock." At half-past six he describes the coming of the grand armada and the expectant scene in these words: "The *Block Island* came down from Norwich with every square foot of her three decks occupied, the *Elm City* brought a mass of Yale sympathizers from New Haven, and the big *City of New*

York filled her long saloon-deck with New London spectators. A special train of eighteen cars came up from New Haven, a blue flag fluttering from every window. The striking contrast to the life and bustle of the lower end of the course was the quiet river at the starting-point. The college launches, the huge tug *America*, the press-boat *Manhasset*, loaded with correspondents, the tug *Burnside*, swathed in crimson by her charter party of Harvard men, and the steam-yacht *Norma*, gay with party-colored bunting, floated idly up-stream, waiting for the start. The long train of twenty-five observation-cars stood quietly by the river-side, its occupants closely watching the boat-houses across the river."

Did any fleet of steamers solid with eager spectators, or special train of eighteen cars, or long train of twenty-five observation-cars, a vast, enthusiastic multitude, ever arrive at any college upon any Commencement Day in Philip Slingsby's time to greet with prolonged roars of cheers and frenzied excitement the surpassing eloquence of Salutatorian Smith, or the melting pathos of Valedictorian Jones? Did ever—for so we read in the veracious history of a day, the newspaper—did ever a college town resound with "a perfect babel of noises" from eight in the summer evening until three in the summer morning, the town lighted with burning tar-barrels and blazing with fireworks, the chimes ringing, and ten thousand people hastening to the illuminated station to receive the victors in triumph—because Brown had vanquished the calculus, or Jones discovered a comet, or Robinson translated the *Daily Gong and Gas Blower* into the purest Choctaw? In a word, was such tumult of acclamation—even the President himself swinging his reverend hat, and the illustrious alumni, far and near, when the glad tidings were told, beaming with joyful complacency, like Mr. Pickwick going down the slide, while Samivel Weller adjured him and the company to keep the pot a-bilin'—ever produced by any scholastic performance or success or triumph whatever?

Echo undoubtedly answers No; and she asks, also, whether in such a competition, when the appeal is to youth, eager, strong, combative, full of physical impulse and prowess, in the time of romantic enjoyment and heroic susceptibility, study is not heavily handicapped, and books at a sorry disadvantage with boats. This is what Echo distinctly inquiries; and what answer shall be made to Echo? Who is the real hero to young Slingsby, who has just fitted himself to enter college—the victor in the boat-race or the noblest scholar of them all? The answer seems to be given unconsciously in the statement that the number of students applying for entrance is notably larger when the college has scored an athletic victory. But this answer is not wholly satisfactory. There may be an observable coincidence, but young men usually prepare themselves to enter a particular college, and do not await the result of boat-races.

But the fact remains that the true college hero of to-day is the victor in games and sports, not in studies; and it is not unnatural that it should be so. It is partly a reaction of feeling against the old notion that a scholar is an invalid, and that a boy must be down in his muscle because he is up in his mathematics. But, as Lincoln said in his debate with Douglas, it does not follow, because I think that innocent men should have equal rights, that I wish my daughter to marry a negro. It does not follow, because the sound mind should be lodged in a sound body, that the care of the body should become the main, and virtually the exclusive, interest.

Yet that this is now somewhat the prevailing tendency of average feeling is undeniable, and it is a tendency to be considered by intelligent collegians themselves. For the true academic prizes are spiritual, not material; and the heroes for college emulation are not the gladiators, but the sages and poets of the ancient day and of all time. The men that the college remembers and cherishes are not ball-players, and boat-racers, and high-jumpers, and boxers, and fencers, and heroes of single-stick, good fellows as they are, but the patriots and scholars and poets and orators and philosophers. Three cheers for brawn, but three times three for brain!

(*September*, 1887)

HAZING

As if a bell had rung, and the venerable dormitories and halls upon the green were pouring forth a crowd of youth loitering towards the recitation-room, the Easy Chair, like a college professor, meditating serious themes, and with a grave purpose, steps to the lecture-desk. It begins by asking the young gentlemen who have loitered into the room, and are now seated, what they think of bullying boys and hunting cats and tying kettles to a dog's tail, and seating a comrade upon tacks with the point upward. Undoubtedly they reply, with dignified nonchalance, that it is all child's play and contemptible. Undoubtedly, young gentlemen, answers the professor, and, to multiply Nathan's remark to David, You are the men!

As American youth you cherish wrathful scorn for the English boy who makes another boy his fag, and you express a sneering pity for the boy who consents to fag. You have read *Dr. Birch and His Young Friends*, and you would like to break the head of Master Hewlett, who shies his shoe at the poor shivering, craven Nightingale, and you justly remark that close observation of John Bull seems to warrant the conclusion that the nature of his bovine ancestor is still far from eliminated from his descendant. And what is the secret of your feeling? Simply that you hate bullying. Why, then, young gentlemen, do you bully?

You retort perhaps that fagging is unknown in America, and that high-spirited youth would not tolerate it. But permit the professor to tell you what is not unknown in America: a crowd of older young gentlemen surrounding one younger fellow, forcing him to do disagreeable and disgusting things, pouring cold water down his back, making a fool of him to his personal injury, he being solitary, helpless, and abused—all this is not unknown in America, young gentlemen. But it is all very different from what we have been accustomed to consider American. If we would morally define or paraphrase the word America, I think we should say fair-play. That is what it means. That is what the Brownist Puritans, the precursors of the Plymouth Pilgrims, left England to secure. They did not bring it indeed, at least in all its fulness, across the sea. Let us say, young gentlemen, that its potentiality, its possibility, rather than its actuality, stepped out of the *Mayflower* upon Plymouth Rock. But from the moment of its landing it has been asserting itself. You need not say "Baptist" and "Quaker." I understand it and allow for it all. But fair-play has prevailed over ecclesiastical hatred and over personal slavery, and what are called the new questions—corporate power, monopoly, capital, and labor—are only new forms of the old effort to secure fair-play.

Now the petty bullying of hazing and the whole system of college tyranny is a most contemptible denial of fair-play. It is a disgrace to the American name, and when you stop in the wretched business to sneer at English fagging you merely advertise the beam in your own eyes. It is not possible, surely, that any honorable young gentleman now attending to the lecture of the professor really supposes that there is any fun or humor or joke in this form of college bullying. Turn to your *Evelina* and see what was accounted humorous, what passed for practical joking, in Miss Burney's time, at the end of the last century. It is not difficult to imagine Dr. Johnson, who greatly delighted in *Evelina*, supposing the intentional upsetting into the ditch of the old French lady in the carriage to be a joke. For a man who unconsciously has made so much fun for others as "the great lexicographer," Dr. Johnson seems to have been curiously devoid of a sense of humor. But he was a genuine Englishman of his time, a true John Bull, and the fun of the John Bull of that time, recorded in the novels and traditions, was entirely bovine.

The bovine or brutal quality is by no means wholly worked out of the blood even yet. The taste for pugilism, or the pummelling of the human frame into a jelly by the force of fisticuffs, as a form of enjoyment or entertainment, is a relapse into barbarism. It is the instinct of the tiger still surviving in the white cat transformed into the princess. I will not call it, young gentlemen, the fond return of Melusina to the gambols of the mermaid, or Undine's momentary unconsciousness of a soul, because these are poetic and pathetic suggestions. The prize-ring is disgusting and inhuman, but at least it is a voluntary encounter of two individuals. But college bullying is unredeemed brutality. It is the extinction of Dr. Jekyll in Mr. Hyde. It is not humorous, nor manly, nor generous, nor decent. It is bald and vulgar cruelty, and no class in college should feel itself worthy of the respect of others, or respect itself, until it has searched out all offenders of this kind who disgrace it, and banished them to the remotest Coventry.

The meanest and most cowardly fellows in college may shine most in hazing. The generous and manly men despise it. There are noble and inspiring ways for working off the high spirits of youth: games which are rich in poetic tradition; athletic exercises which mould the young Apollo. To drive a young fellow upon the thin ice, through which he breaks, and by the icy submersion becomes at last a cripple, helpless with inflammatory rheumatism—surely no young man in his senses thinks this to be funny, or anything but an unspeakable outrage. Or to overwhelm with terror a comrade of sensitive temperament until his mind reels—imps of Satan might delight in such a revel, but young Americans!—never, young gentlemen, never!

The hazers in college are the men who have been bred upon dime novels and the prize-ring—in spirit, at least, if not in fact—to whom the training and instincts of the gentleman are unknown. That word is one of the most precious among English words. The man who is justly entitled to it wears a diamond of the purest lustre. Tennyson, in sweeping the whole range of tender praise for his dead friend Arthur Hallam, says that he bore without abuse the grand old name of gentleman. "Without abuse"—that is the wise qualification. The name may be foully abused. I read in the morning's paper, young gentlemen, a pitiful story of a woman trying to throw herself from the bridge. You may recall one like it in Hood's "Bridge of Sighs." The report was headed: "To hide her shame." "*Her* shame?" Why, gentlemen, at that very moment, in bright and bewildering rooms, the arms of Lothario and Lovelace were encircling your sisters' waists in the intoxicating waltz. These men go unwhipped of an epithet. They are even enticed and flattered by the mothers of the girls. But, for all that, they do not bear without abuse the name of gentleman, and Sidney and Bayard and Hallam would scorn their profanation and betrayal of the name.

The soul of the gentleman, what is it? Is it anything but kindly and thoughtful respect for others, helping the helpless, succoring the needy, befriending the friendless and forlorn, doing justice, requiring fair-play, and withstanding with every honorable means the bully of the church and caucus, of the drawing-room, the street, the college? Respect, young gentlemen, like charity, begins at home. Only the man who respects himself can be a gentleman, and no gentleman will willingly annoy, torment, or injure another.

There will be no further recitation today. The class is dismissed.

(*March*, 1888)

THE SOUL OF THE GENTLEMAN

To find a satisfactory definition of gentleman is as difficult as to discover the philosopher's stone; and yet if we may not say just what a gentleman is, we can certainly say what he is not. We may affirm indisputably that a man, however rich, and of however fine a title in countries where rank is acknowledged, if he behave selfishly, coarsely, and indecently, is not a gentleman. "From which, young gentlemen, it follows," as the good professor used to say at college, as he emerged from a hopeless labyrinth of postulates and preliminaries an hour long, that the guests who abused the courtesy of their hosts, upon the late transcontinental trip to drive the golden spike, may have been persons of social eminence, but were in no honorable sense gentlemen.

It is undoubtedly a difficult word to manage. But gentlemanly conduct and ungentlemanly conduct are expressions which are perfectly intelligible, and that fact shows that there is a distinct standard in every intelligent mind by which behavior is measured. To say that a man was born a gentleman means not at all that he is courteous, refined, and intelligent, but only that he was born of a family whose circumstances at some time had been easy and agreeable, and which belonged to a traditionally "good society." But such a man may be false and mean, and ignorant and coarse. Is he a gentleman because he was born such? On the other hand, the child of long generations of ignorant and laborious boors may be humane, honorable, and modest, but with total ignorance of the usages of good society. He may be as upright as Washington, as unselfish as Sidney, as brave as Bayard, as modest as Falkland. But he may also outrage all the little social proprieties. Is he a gentleman because he is honest and modest and humane? In describing Lovelace, should we not say that he was a gentleman? Should we naturally say so of Burns? But, again, is it not a joke to describe George IV. as a gentleman, while it would be impossible to deny the name to Major Dobbin?

The catch, however, is simple. Using the same word, we interchange its different meanings. To say that a man is born a gentleman is to say that he was born under certain social conditions. To say in commendation or description of a man that he is a gentleman, or gentlemanly, is to say that he has certain qualities of character or manner which are wholly independent of the circumstances of his family or training. In the latter case, we speak of individual and personal qualities; in the former, we speak of external conditions. In the one case we refer to the man himself; in the other, to certain circumstances around him. The quality which is called gentlemanly is that which, theoretically, and often actually, distinguishes the person who is born in a certain social position. It describes the manner in which such a person ought to behave.

Behavior, however, can be imitated. Therefore, neither the fact of birth under certain conditions, nor a certain ease and grace and charm of manner, certify the essential character of gentleman. Lovelace had the air and breeding of a gentleman like Don Giovanni; he was familiar with polite society; he was refined and pleasing and fascinating in manner. Even the severe Astarte could not call him a boor. She does not know a gentleman, probably, more gentlemanly than Lovelace. She must, then, admit that she can not arbitrarily deny Lovelace to be a gentleman because he is a libertine, or because he is false, or mean, or of a coarse mind. She may, indeed, insist that only upright and honorable men of refined mind and manner are gentlemen, and she may also maintain that only men of truly lofty and royal souls are princes; but there will still remain crowds of immoral gentlemen and unworthy kings.

The persons who abused the generous courtesy of the Northern Pacific trip were gentlemen in one sense, and not in the other. They were gentlemen so far as they could not help themselves, but they were not gentlemen in what depended upon their own will. According to the story, they did not even imitate the conduct of gentlemen, and Astarte must admit that they belonged to the large class of ungentlemanly gentlemen.

(December, 1883)

THEATRE MANNERS

An admirable actress said the other day that the audience in the theatre was probably little aware how much its conduct affected the performance. A listless, whispering, uneasy house makes a distracted and ineffective play. To an orator, or an actor, or an artist of any kind who appeals personally to the public, nothing is so fatal as indifference. In the original Wallack's Theatre, many years ago, the Easy Chair was one of a party in a stage-box during a fine performance of one of the plays in which the acting of the manager was most effective. It was a gay party, and with the carelessness of youth it made merry while the play went on. As the box was directly upon the stage, the merriment was a gross discourtesy, although unintentional, both to the actors and to the audience; and at last the old Wallack, still gayly playing his part, moved towards the box, and without turning his head, in a voice audible to the offenders but not to the rest of the audience, politely reminded the thoughtless group that they were seriously disturbing the play. There was some indignation in the box, but the rebuke was courteous and richly deserved. Nothing is more unpardonable than such disturbance.

During this winter a gentleman at one of the theatres commented severely upon the loud talking of a party of ladies, which prevented his enjoyment of the play, and when the gentleman attending the ladies retorted warmly, the disturbed gentleman resorted to the wild justice of a blow. There was an altercation, a publication in the newspapers, and finally an apology and a reconciliation. But it is to be hoped that there was some good result from the incident. A waggish clergyman once saw a pompous clerical brother march quite to the head of the aisle of a crowded church to find a seat, with an air of expectation that all pew-doors would fly open at his approach. But as every seat was full, and nobody stirred, the crestfallen brother was obliged to retrace his steps. As he retreated by the pew, far down the aisle, where the clerical wag was sitting, that pleasant man leaned over the door, and greeted his comrade with the sententious whisper, "May it be sanctified to you, dear brother!" Every right-minded man will wish the same blessing to the rebuke of the loud-talking maids and youths in theatres and concert-halls, whose conversation, however lively, is not the entertainment which their neighbors have come to hear.

Two or three winters ago the Easy Chair applauded the conduct of Mr. Thomas, who, at the head of his orchestra, was interrupted in the midst of a concert in Washington by the entry of a party, which advanced towards the front of the hall with much chattering and rustling, and seated themselves and continued the disturbance. The orchestra was in full career, but Thomas rapped sharply upon his stand, and brought the performance to an abrupt pause. Then, turning to the audience, he said—and doubtless with evident and natural feeling: "I am afraid that the music interrupts the conversation." The remark was greeted with warm and general applause; and, waiting until entire silence was restored, the conductor raised his baton again, and the performance ended without further interruption.

The Easy Chair improved the occasion to preach a short sermon upon bad manners in public places. But to its great surprise it was severely rebuked some time afterward by Cleopatra herself, who said, with some feeling, that she had two reasons for complaint. The first was, that her ancient friend the Easy Chair should place her in the pillory of its public animadversion; and the other was, that the Easy Chair should gravely defend such conduct as that of Mr. Thomas. No remonstrance could be more surprising and nothing more unexpected than that Cleopatra should differ in opinion upon such a point. To the personal aspect of the matter the Easy Chair could say only that it had never heard who the offenders were, and that it declined to believe that Cleopatra herself could ever be guilty of such conduct. Her Majesty then explained that she was not guilty. She was not of the party. But it was composed of friends of hers who seated themselves near her, and when the words of Mr. Thomas concentrated the gaze of the audience upon the disturbers of the peace, her Majesty, known to everybody, was supposed to be the ringleader of the *émeute*. The story at once flew abroad, upon the wings of those swift birds of prey—as she called them—the Washington correspondents, and she was mentioned by name as the chief offender.

It was not difficult to persuade the most placable of queens that the Easy Chair could not have intended a personal censure. But the Chair could not agree that Thomas's conduct was unjustifiable. Cleopatra urged that the conductor of an orchestra at a concert is not responsible for the behavior of the audience. An audience, she said, can take care of itself, and it is an unwarrantable impertinence for a conductor to arrest the performance because he is irritated by a noise of whispering voices or of slamming doors. "I saw you, Mr. Easy Chair," she said, "on the evening of Rachel's first performance in this country. What would you have thought if she had stopped short in the play—it was Corneille's *Les Horaces*, you remember—because she was annoyed by the rustling of the leaves of a thousand books of the play which the audience turned over at the same moment?"

The Easy Chair declined to step into the snare which was plainly set in its sight. It would not accept an illustration as an argument. The enjoyment at a concert, it contended, for which the audience has paid in advance, and to which it is entitled, depends upon conditions of silence and order which it can not itself maintain without serious disturbance. It may indeed cry "Hush!" and "Put him out!" but not only would that cry be of doubtful effect, but experience proves that a concert audience will not raise it. If the audience were left to itself, it would permit late arrivals, and all the disturbance of chatter and movement. To twist the line of Goldsmith, those who came to pray would be at the mercy of those who came to scoff; and such mercy is merciless. The conductor stands *in loco parentis*. He is the *advocatus angeli*. He does for the audience what it would not do for itself. He protects it against its own fatal good-nature. He insists that it shall receive what it has paid for, and he will deal with disturbers as they deserve. The audience, conscious of its own good-humored impotence, recognizes at once its protector, and gladly applauds him for doing for it what it has not the nerve to do for itself. No audience whose rights were defended as Thomas defended those of his Washington audience ever resented the defence.

"No," responded Cleopatra, briskly; "the same imbecility prevents."

"Very well; then such an audience plainly needs a strong and resolute leadership; and that is precisely what Thomas supplied. A crowd is always grateful to the man who will do what everybody in the crowd feels ought to be done, but what no individual is quite ready to undertake."

When Cleopatra said that an audience is quite competent to take care of itself, her remark was natural, for she instinctively conceived the audience as herself extended into a thousand persons. Such an audience would certainly be capable of dispensing with any mentor or guide. But when the Easy Chair asked her if she was annoyed by the chattering interruption which Thomas rebuked, she replied that of course she was annoyed. Yet when she was further asked if she cried "Hush!" or resorted to any means whatever to quell the disturbance, the royal lady could not help smiling as she answered, "I did not," and the Easy Chair retorted, "Yet an audience is capable of protecting itself!"

Meanwhile, whatever the conductor or the audience may or may not do, nothing is more vulgar than audible conversation, or any other kind of disturbance, during a concert. Sometimes it may be mere thoughtlessness;

sometimes boorishness, the want of the fine instinct which avoids occasioning any annoyance; but usually it is due to a desire to attract attention and to affect superiority to the common interest. It is, indeed, mere coarse ostentation, like wearing diamonds at a hotel table or a purple velvet train in the street. If the audience had the courage which Cleopatra attributed to it, that part which was annoyed by the barbarians who chatter and disturb would at once suppress the annoyance by an emphatic and unmistakable hiss. If this were the practice in public assemblies, such incidents as that at the Washington concert would be unknown. Until it is the practice, even were Cleopatra's self the offender, every self-respecting conductor who has a proper sense of his duties to the audience will do with its sincere approval what Mr. Thomas did.

(*April*, 1883)

WOMAN'S DRESS

The American who sits in a street omnibus or railroad-car and sees a young woman whose waist is pinched to a point that makes her breathing mere panting and puffing, and whose feet are squeezed into shoes with a high heel in the middle of the sole, which compels her to stump and hobble as she tries to walk, should be very wary of praising the superiority of European and American civilization to that of the East. The grade of civilization which squeezes a waist into deformity is not, in that respect at least, superior to that which squeezes a foot into deformity. It is in both instances a barbarous conception alike of beauty and of the function of woman. The squeezed waist and the squeezed foot equally assume that distortion of the human frame may be beautiful, and that helpless idleness is the highest sphere of woman.

But the imperfection of our Western civilization shows itself in more serious forms involving women. The promiscuous herding of men and women prisoners in jails, the opposition to reformatories and penitentiaries exclusively for women, and, in general, the failure to provide, as a matter of course, women attendants and women nurses for all women prisoners and patients, is a signal illustration of a low tone of civilization. The most revolting instance of this abuse was the discovery during the summer that the patients in a woman's insane hospital in New Orleans were bathed by male attendants.

It should not need such outrages to apprise us of the worth of the general principle that humanity and decency require that in all public institutions women should be employed in the care of women. A wise proposition during the year to provide women at the police-stations for the examination of women who are arrested failed to become law. It is hard, upon the merits of the proposal, to understand why. Women who are arrested may be criminals, or drunkards, or vagabonds, or insane, or witless, or sick. But whatever the reason of the arrest, there can be no good reason whatever, in a truly civilized community, that a woman taken under such circumstances should be abandoned to personal search and examination by the kind of men to whom that business is usually allotted. The surest sign of the civilization of any community is its treatment of women, and the progress of our civilization is shown by the constant amelioration of that condition. But the unreasonable and even revolting circumstances of much of the public treatment of them may wisely modify ecstasies over our vast superiority.

The squeezed waists and other tokens of the kind show that our civilization has not yet outgrown the conception of the most meretricious epochs, that woman exists for the delight of man, and is meant to be a kind of decorated appendage of his life, while the men attendants and men nurses of women prisoners and patients show a most uncivilized disregard of the just instincts of sex. We are far from asserting that therefore the position of women in this country is to be likened to their position in China, where the contempt of men denied them souls, or to that among savage tribes, where they are treated as beasts of burden. But because we are not wallowing in the Slough of Despond, it does not follow that we are sitting in the House Beautiful. The traveller who has climbed to the *mer de glace* at Chamouni, and sees the valley wide outstretched far below him, sees also far above him the awful sunlit dome of "Sovran Blanc." Whatever point we may have reached, there is still a higher point to gain. Nowhere in the world are women so truly respected as here, nowhere ought they to be more happy than in this country. But that is no reason that the New Orleans outrage should be possible, while the same good sense and love of justice which have removed so many barriers to fair-play for women should press on more cheerfully than ever to remove those that remain.

(*December*, 1882)

SECRET SOCIETIES

The melancholy death of young Mr. Leggett, a student at the Cornell University, has undoubtedly occasioned a great deal of thought in every college in the country upon secret societies. Professor Wilder, of Cornell, has written a very careful and serious letter, in which he strongly opposes them, plainly stating their great disadvantages, and citing the order of Jesuits as the most powerful and thoroughly organized of all secret associations, and therefore the one in which their character and tendency may best be observed. The debate recalls the history of the Antimasonic excitement in this country, which is, however, seldom mentioned in recent years, so that the facts may not be familiar to the reader.

In the year 1826 William Morgan, living in Batavia, in the western part of New York, near Buffalo, was supposed to intend the publication of a book which would reveal the secrets of Masonry. The Masons in the vicinity were angry, and resolved to prevent the publication, and made several forcible but ineffective attempts for that purpose. On the 11th of September, 1826, a party of persons from Canandaigua came to Batavia and procured the arrest of Morgan upon a criminal charge, and he was carried to Canandaigua for examination. He was acquitted, but was immediately arrested upon a civil process, upon which an execution was issued, and he was imprisoned in the jail at Canandaigua. The next evening he was discharged at the instance of those who had caused his arrest, and was taken from the jail after nine o'clock in the evening. Those who had obtained the discharge instantly seized him, gagged and bound him, and throwing him into a carriage, hurried off to Rochester. By relays of horses and by different hands he was borne along, until he was lodged in the magazine of Fort Niagara, at the mouth of the Niagara River.

The circumstances of his arrest, and those that had preceded it, had aroused and inflamed the minds of the people in Batavia and the neighborhood. A committee was appointed at a public meeting to ascertain all the facts, and to bring to justice any criminals that might be found. They could discover only that Morgan had been seized upon his discharge in Canandaigua and hurried off towards Rochester; but beyond that, nothing. The excitement deepened and spread. A great crime had apparently been committed, and it was hidden in absolute secrecy. Other meetings were held in other towns, and other committees were appointed, and both meetings and committees were composed of men of both political parties. Investigation showed that Masons only were implicated in the crime, and that scarcely a Mason aided the inquiry; that many Masons ridiculed and even justified the offence; that the committees were taunted with their inability to procure the punishment of the offenders in courts where judges, sheriffs, juries, and witnesses were Masons; that witnesses disappeared; that the committees were reviled; and gradually Masonry itself was held responsible for the mysterious doom of Morgan.

The excitement became a frenzy. The Masons were hated and denounced as the Irish were in London after the "Irish night," or the Roman Catholics during the Titus Oates fury. In January, 1827, some of those who had been arrested were tried, and it was hoped that the evidence at their trials would clear the mystery. But they pleaded guilty, and this hope was baffled. Meanwhile a body of delegates from the various committees met at Lewiston to ascertain the fate of Morgan, and they discovered that in or near the magazine in which he had been confined he had been put to death. His book, with its revelations, had been published, and what was not told was, of course, declared to be infinitely worse than the actual disclosures. The excitement now became political. It was alleged that Masonry held itself superior to the laws, and that Masons were more loyal to their Masonic oaths than to their duty as citizens. Masonry, therefore, was held to be a fatal foe to the government and to the country, which must be destroyed; and in several town-meetings in Genesee and Monroe counties, in the spring of 1827, Masons, as such, were excluded from office. At the next general election the Antimasons nominated a separate ticket, and they carried the counties of Genesee, Monroe, Livingston, Orleans, and Niagara against both the great parties. A State organization followed, and in the election of 1830 the Antimasonic candidate, Francis Granger, was adopted by the National Republicans, and received one hundred and twenty thousand votes, against one hundred and twenty-eight thousand for Mr. Throop. From a State organization the Antimasons became a national party, and in 1832 nominated William Wirt for the presidency. The Antimasonic electoral ticket was adopted by the National Republicans, and the union became the Whig party, which, in 1838, elected Mr. Seward Governor of New York, and in 1840 General Harrison President of the United States.

The spring of this triumphant political movement was hostility to a secret society. Many of the most distinguished political names of Western New York, including Millard Fillmore, William H. Seward, Thurlow Weed, Francis Granger, James Wadsworth, George W. Patterson, were associated with it. And as the larger portion of the Whig party was merged in the Republican, the dominant party of to-day has a certain lineal descent from the feelings aroused by the abduction of Morgan from the jail at Canandaigua. And as his disappearance and the odium consequent upon it stigmatized Masonry, so that it lay for a long time moribund, and although revived in later years, cannot hope to regain its old importance, so the death of young Leggett is likely to wound fatally the system of college secret societies.

The young man was undergoing initiation into a secret society. He was blind-folded, and two companions were leading him along the edge of a cliff over a deep ravine, when the earth gave way, or they slipped and fell from the precipice, and Leggett was so injured that he died in two hours. There was no allegation or suspicion of blame. There was, indeed, an attempt of some enemies of the Cornell University—a hostility due either to supposed conflict of interests or sectarian jealousy—to stigmatize the institution, but it failed instantly and utterly. Indeed, General Leggett, of the Patent-office in Washington, the father of the unfortunate youth, at once wrote a very noble and touching letter to shield the university and the companions of his son from blame or responsibility. He would not allow his grief to keep him silent when a word could avert injustice, and his modest magnanimity won for his sorrow the tender sympathy of all who read his letter.

Every collegian knows that there is no secrecy whatever in what is called a secret society. Everybody knows, not in particular, but in general, that its object is really "good-fellowship," with the charm of mystery added. Everybody knows—for the details of such societies in all countries are essentially the same—that there are certain practical jokes of initiation— tossings in blankets, layings in coffins, dippings in cold water, stringent catechisms, moral exhortations, with darkness and sudden light and mysterious voices from forms invisible, and then mystic signs and clasps and mottoes, "the whole to conclude" with the best supper that the treasury can afford. Literary brotherhood, philosophic fraternity, intellectual emulation, these are the noble names by which the youth deceive themselves and allure the Freshmen; but the real business of the society is to keep the secret, and to get all the members possible from the entering class.

Each society, of course, gets "the best fellows." Every touter informs the callow Freshman that all men of character and talent hasten to join his society, and impresses the fresh imagination with the names of the famous honorary members. The Freshman, if he be acute—and he is more so every year—naturally wonders how the youth, who are undeniably commonplace in the daily intercourse of college, should become such lofty beings in the hall of a secret society; or, more probably, he thinks of nothing but the sport or the mysterious incentive to a studious and higher life which the society is to furnish. He feels the passionate curiosity of the neophyte. He is smitten with the zeal of the hermetical philosophy. He would learn more than Rosicrucian lore. That is a vision soon dispelled. But the earnest curiosity changes into *esprit du corps,* and the mischief is that the secrecy and the society feeling are likely to take precedence of the really desirable motives in college. There is a hundredfold greater zeal to obtain members than there is generous rivalry among the societies to carry off the true college honors. And if the purpose be admirable, why, as Professor Wilder asks, the secrecy? What more can the secret society do for the intellectual or social training of the student than the open society? Has any secret society in an American college done, or can it do, more for the intelligent and ambitious young man than the Union Debating Society at the English Cambridge University, or the similar club at Oxford? There Macaulay, Gladstone, the Austins, Charles Buller, Tooke, Ellis, and the long illustrious list of noted and able Englishmen were trained, and in the only way that manly minds can be trained, by open, free, generous rivalry and collision. The member of a secret society in college is really confined, socially and intellectually, to its membership, for it is found that the secret gradually supplant the open societies. But that membership depends upon luck, not upon merit, while it has the capital disadvantage of erecting false standards of measurement, so that the *Mu Nu* man cannot be just to the hero of *Zeta Eta.* The secrecy is a spice that overbears the food. The mystic paraphernalia is a relic of the baby-house, which a generous youth disdains.

There is, indeed, an agreeable sentiment in the veiled friendship of the secret society which every social nature understands. But as students are now becoming more truly "men" as they enter college, because of the higher standard of requirement, it is probable that the glory of the secret society is already waning, and that the allegiance of the older universities to the open arenas of frank and manly intellectual contests, involving no expense, no dissipation, and no perilous temptation, is returning. At least there will now be an urgent question among many of the best men in college whether it ought not to return.

(*January,* 1874)

TOBACCO AND HEALTH

We do not know if readers upon your side of the water have watched with any interest the present violent onslaught in both England and France upon the use of tobacco. Sir Benjamin Brodie (of London) has declared strongly against its use; and at a recent meeting at Edinburgh of the British Anti-Tobacco Society, Professor Miller, moving the first resolution, as follows: "That as the constituent principles which tobacco contains are highly poisonous, the practices of smoking and snuffing tend in a variety of ways to injure the physical and mental constitution," continued: "No man who was a hard smoker had a steady hand. But not only had it a debilitating and paralyzing effect; but he could tell of patients who were completely paralyzed in their limbs by inveterate smoking. He might tell of a patient of his who brought on an attack of paralysis by smoking; who was cured, indeed, by simple means enough, accompanied with the complete discontinuance of the practice; but who afterwards took to it again, and got a new attack of paralysis; and who could now play with himself, as it were, because when he wanted a day's paralysis or an approach to it, he had nothing to do but to indulge more or less freely with the weed. Only the other day, the French—among whom the practice was carried even to a greater extent than with us—made an estimate of its effects in their schools, and academies, and colleges. They took the young men attending these institutions, classified them into those who smoked habitually and those who did not, and estimated their physical and intellectual standing, perhaps their moral standing too, but he could not say. The result was, that they found that those who did not smoke were the stronger lads and better scholars, were altogether more reputable people, and more useful members of society than those who habitually used the drug. What was the consequence? Louis Napoleon—one of the good things which he had done—instantly issued an edict that no smoking should be permitted in any school, college, or academy. In one day he put out about 30,000 pipes in Paris alone. Let our young smokers put that in their pipe and smoke it." The resolution was agreed to.

Is it possible to entertain the idea that Louis Napoleon has increased the tax on tobacco, latterly, very largely, in the hope of discouraging its use, and so contributing to the weal of the nation? If so, it would illustrate one of the beautiful uses of despotic privilege.

(*February*, 1861)

TOBACCO AND MANNERS

I

The "old school" of manners has fallen into disrepute. Sir Charles Grandison is a comical rather than a courtly figure to this generation; and the man whose manners may be described as Grandisonian is usually called a pompous and grandiloquent old prig. Certainly the elaborately dressed gentleman speaking to a lady only with polished courtesy of phrase, and avoiding in her presence all coarse words and acts, handing her in the minuet with inexpressible grace and deference, and showing an exquisite homage in every motion, was a very different figure from the gentleman in a shooting-jacket or morning sack "chaffing" a lady with the freshest slang, and smoking in her face. They are undeniably different, and the later figure is wholly free from Grandisonian elegance and elaboration. But is he much more truly a gentleman? Is he our Sidney, our Chevalier Bayard, our Admirable Crichton? Is that refined consideration and gentle deference, which is the flower of courtesy, an old-fashioned folly?

The overwrought politeness is made very ridiculous upon the stage, and Richardson is undoubtedly hard reading for the general consumer of novels. It is true, also, that fine morals do not always go with fine manners, and that Lovelace had a fascination of address which John Knox lacked. The chaff and slang of the Bayard of to-day are at least decent, and his morals probably purer than those of the courtly and punctilious old Sir Roger de Coverleys. Possibly; but it has been wisely said that hypocrisy is the homage paid by vice to virtue. The good manners of a bad man are a rich dress upon a diseased body. They are the graceful form of a vase full of dirty water. The liquid may be poisonous, but the vessel is beautiful. Some of the worst Lotharios in the world have a personal charm which is irresistible. Many a stately compliment was paid by a graciously bowing satyr in laced velvet coat and periwig, at the court of Louis the Great, and paid for the basest purpose; but the grace and the courtesy were borrowed, like plumage of living hues to deck carrion. They were not a part of the baseness, and you do not escape dirty water by breaking the vase. If the older morals were worse than the new, and the older manners were better, cannot we who live to-day, and who may have everything, combine the new morals and the old manners?

We can spare some elaboration of form, but we cannot safely spare the substance of refined deference. If Romeo be permitted to treat Juliet as hostlers are supposed to treat barmaids, and as the heroes of Fielding and Smollett treat Abigails upon a journey, they will both lose self-respect and mutual respect. It was a wise father who said to his son, "Beware of the woman who allows you to kiss her." The woman who does not require of a man the form of respect invites him to discard the substance. And there is one violation of the form which is recent and gross, and might be well cited as a striking illustration of the decay of manners. It is the practice of smoking in the society of ladies in public places, whether driving, or walking, or sailing, or sitting. There are *preux chevaliers* who would be honestly amazed if they were told they did not behave like gentlemen, who, sitting with a lady on a hotel piazza, or strolling on a public park, whip out a cigarette, light it, and puff as tranquilly as if they were alone in their rooms. Or a young man comes alone upon the deck of a steamer, where throngs of ladies are sitting, and blows clouds of tobacco smoke in their faces, without even remarking that tobacco is disagreeable to some people. This is not, indeed, one of the seven deadly sins, but a man who unconcernedly sings false betrays that he has no ear for music, and the man who smokes in this way shows that he is not quite a gentleman.

But some ladies smoke? Yes, and some ladies drink liquor. Does that mend the matter? The Easy Chair has seen a lady at the head of her own table smoking a fine cigar. You will see a great many highly dressed women in Paris smoking cigarettes. Does all this change the situation? Does this make it more gentlemanly to smoke with a lady beside you in a carriage, or upon a bench on the piazza? But some ladies like the odor of a cigar? Not many; and the taste of those who sincerely do so cannot justify the habit of promiscuous puffing in their presence. The intimacy of domesticity is governed by other rules; but a gentleman smoking would hardly enter his own drawing-room, where other ladies sat with his wife, without a word of apology. The Easy Chair is no King James, and is more likely to issue blasts of tobacco than blasts against it. But King James belonged to a very selfish sex—a sex which seems often to suppose that its indulgences and habits are to be tenderly tolerated, for no other reason than that they are its habits. Therefore the young woman must defend herself by showing plainly that she prohibits the intrusion of which, if suffered, she is really the victim. In other times the Easy Chair has seen the lovely Laura Matilda unwilling to refuse to dance with the partner who had bespoken her hand for the german, although when he presented himself he was plainly flown with wine. The Easy Chair has seen the hapless, foolish maid encircled by those Bacchic arms, and then a headlong whirl and dash down the room, ending in the promiscuous overthrow and downfall of maid, Bacchus, and musicians.

If in the Grandisonian day the morals were wanting, it was something to have the manners. They at least were to the imagination a memory and a prophecy. They recalled the idyllic age when fine manners expressed fine feelings, and they foretold the return of Astræa to her ancient haunts. Here is young Adonis dreaming of a four-in-hand and a yacht, like any other gentleman. Let us hope that he knows the test of a gentleman not to be the ownership of blood-horses and a unique drag, but perfect courtesy founded upon fine human feeling—that rare and indescribable gentleness and consideration which rests upon manner as lightly as the bloom upon a fruit. It may be imitated, as gold and diamonds are. But no counterfeit can harm it; and, Adonis, it is incompatible with smoking in a lady's face, even if she acquiesces.

(*September*, 1879)

II

Apollodorus came in the other morning and announced to the Easy Chair that it had been made by common consent arbiter of a dispute in a circle of young men. "The question," said he, "is not a new one in itself, but it constantly recurs, for it is the inquiry under what conditions a gentleman may smoke in the presence of ladies."

The Easy Chair replied that it could not answer more pertinently than in the words of the famous Princess Emilia, who, upon being asked by a youth who was attending her in a promenade around the garden, "What should you say if a gentleman asked to smoke as he walked with you?" replied, "It is not supposable, for no gentleman would propose it."

Naturally that youth did not venture to light even a cigarette. Emilia had parried his question so dexterously that, although the rebuke was stinging, he could not even pretend to be offended. His question was merely a form of saying, "I am about to smoke, and what have you to say?" That he asked the question was evidence of a lingering persuasion, inherited from an ancestry of gentlemen, that it was not seemly to puff tobacco smoke around a lady with whom he was walking.

Apollodorus was silent for a moment, as if reflecting whether this anecdote was to be regarded as a general judgment of the arbiter that a gentleman will never smoke in the presence of a lady. But the Easy Chair broke in upon his meditation with a question, "If you had a son, should you wish to meet him smoking as he accompanied a lady upon the avenue? or, were you the father of a daughter, should you wish to see her cavalier smoking as he walked by her side? Upon your own theory of what is gentlemanly and courteous and respectful and becoming in the manner of a man towards a woman, should you regard the spectacle with satisfaction?"

"Well," replied Apollodorus, "isn't that rather a high-flying view? When can a man smoke—"

"But you are not answering," interrupted the Easy Chair. "Of two youths walking with your daughter, one of whom was smoking a cigarette, or a cigar, or a pipe, as he attended her, and the other was not smoking, which would seem to you the more gentlemanly?"

"The latter," said Apollodorus, promptly and frankly.

"It appears, then," returned the Easy Chair, assuming the Socratic manner, "that there are circumstances under which a gentleman will not smoke in the presence of a lady. But to answer your question directly, it is not possible to prescribe an exact code, although certain conditions may be definitely stated. For instance, a gentleman will not smoke while walking with a lady in the street. He will not smoke while paying her an evening visit in her drawing-room. He will not smoke while driving with her in the Park."

It is significant of a radical change in manners that such rules can be laid down, because formerly the question could not have arisen. The grandfather of Apollodorus, who was the flower of courtesy, could no more have smoked with a lady with whom he was walking or driving than he could have attended her without a coat or collar. Yet manners change, and the grandfather must not insist that those of his time were best because they were those of his time. It is but a little while since that a gentleman who appeared at a party without gloves would have been a "queer" figure. But now should he wear gloves he would be remarked as unfamiliar with good usage.

It does not argue a decline of courtesy that the Grandisonian compliment and the ineffable bending over a lady's hand and respectful kissing of the finger-tips have yielded to a simpler and less stately manner. The woman of the minuet was not really more respected than the woman of the waltz. However the word gentlemanly may be defined, it will not be questioned that the quality which it describes is sympathetic regard for the feelings of others and the manner which evinces it. The manner, of course, may be counterfeited and put to base uses. To say that Lovelace has a gentlemanly manner is not to say that he is a gentleman, but only that he has caught the trick of a gentleman. To call him or Robert Macaire or Richard Turpin a gentleman is to say only that he behaves as a gentleman behaves. But he is not a gentleman, unless that word describes manners and nothing more.

This is the key to the question of Apollodorus. It is not easy to define a gentleman, but it is perfectly easy to see that in his pleasures and in the little indifferent practices of society the gentleman will do nothing which is disagreeable to others. He certainly will not assume that a personal gratification or indulgence must necessarily be pleasant to others, nor will he make the selfish habits of others a plea for his own.

Apollodorus listened patiently, and then said slowly that he understood the judgment to be that a gentleman would smoke in the presence of ladies only when he knew that it was agreeable to them, but that, as the infinite grace and courtesy of women often led them, as an act of self-denial, to persuade themselves that what others wish to do ought not to annoy them, it was very difficult to know whether the practice was or was not offensive to any particular lady, and therefore—therefore—

The youth seemed to be unable to draw the conclusion.

"Therefore," said the mentor, "it is well to remember the old rule in whist."

"Which is—?" asked Apollodorus.

"When in doubt, trump the trick."

"But what is the special application of that rule to this case?"

"Precisely this, that the doubting smoker should follow the advice of *Punch* to those about to marry."

"Which is—?" asked Apollodorus.

"Don't."

(*September*, 1883)

DUELLING

Twenty-five years ago, at the table of a gentleman whose father had fallen in a duel, the conversation fell upon duelling, and after it had proceeded for some time the host remarked, emphatically, that there were occasions when it was a man's solemn duty to fight. The personal reference was too significant to permit further insistence at that table that duelling was criminal folly, and the subject of conversation was changed.

The host, however, had only reiterated the familiar view of General Hamilton. His plea was, that in the state of public opinion at the time when Burr challenged him, to refuse to fight under circumstances which by the "code of honor" authorized a challenge, was to accept a brand of cowardice and of a want of gentlemanly feeling, which would banish him to a moral and social Coventry, and throw a cloud of discredit upon his family. So Hamilton, one of the bravest men and one of the acutest intellects of his time, permitted a worthless fellow to murder him. Yet there is no doubt that he stated accurately the general feeling of the social circle in which he lived. There was probably not a conspicuous member of that society who was of military antecedents who would not have challenged any man who had said of him what Hamilton had said of Burr. Hamilton disdained explanation or recantation, and the result was accepted as tragical, but in a certain sense inevitable.

Yet that result aroused public sentiment to the atrocity of this barbarous survival of the ordeal of private battle. That one of the most justly renowned of public men, of unsurpassed ability, should be shot to death like a mad dog, because he had expressed the general feeling about an unprincipled schemer, was an exasperating public misfortune. But that he should have been murdered in deference to a practice which was approved in the best society, yet which placed every other valuable life at the mercy of any wily vagabond, was a public peril. From that day to this there has been no duel which could be said to have commanded public sympathy or approval. From the bright June morning, eighty years ago, when Hamilton fell at Weehawken, to the June of this year, when two foolish men shot at each other in Virginia, there has been a steady and complete change of public opinion, and the performance of this year was received with almost universal contempt, and with indignant censure of a dilatory police.

The most celebrated duel in this country since that of Hamilton and Burr was the encounter between Commodores Decatur and Barron, in 1820, near Washington, in which Decatur, like Hamilton, was mortally wounded, and likewise lived but a few hours. The quarrel was one of professional, as Burr's of political, jealousy. But as the only conceivable advantage of the Hamilton duel lay in its arousing the public mind to the barbarity of duelling, the only gain from the Decatur duel was that it confirmed this conviction. In both instances there was an unspeakable shock to the country and infinite domestic anguish. Nothing else was achieved. Neither general manners nor morals were improved, nor was the fame of either combatant heightened, nor public confidence in the men or admiration of their public services increased. In both cases it was a calamity alleviated solely by the resolution which it awakened that such calamities should not occur again.

Such a resolution, indeed, could not at once prevail, and eighteen years after Decatur was killed, Jonathan Cilley, of Maine, was killed in a duel at Washington by William J. Graves, of Kentucky. This event occurred forty-five years ago, but the outcry with which it was received even at that time—one of the newspaper moralists lapsing into rhyme as he deplored the cruel custom which led excellent men to the fatal field,

"where Cilleys meet their Graves" —

and the practical disappearance of Mr. Graves from public life, showed how deep and strong was the public condemnation, and how radically the general view of the duel was changed.

Even in the burning height of the political and sectional animosity of 1856, when Brooks had assaulted Charles Sumner, the challenge of Brooks by some of Sumner's friends met with little public sympathy. During the excitement the Easy Chair met the late Count Gurowski, who was a constant and devoted friend of Mr. Sumner, but an old-world man, with all the hereditary social prejudices of the old world. The count was furious that such a dastardly blow had not been avenged. "Has he no friends?" he exclaimed. "Is there no honor left in your country?" And, as if he would burst with indignant impatience, he shook both his fists in the air, and thundered out, "Good God! will not somebody challenge anybody?"

No, that time is passed. The elderly club dude may lament the decay of the good old code of honor—a word of which he has a very ludicrous conception—as Major Pendennis, when he pulled off his wig, and took out his false teeth, and removed the padded calves of his legs, used to hope that the world was not sinking into shams in its old age. Quarrelling editors may win a morning's notoriety by stealing to the field, furnishing a paragraph for the reporters, and running away from the police. But they gain only the unsavory notoriety of the man in a curled wig and flowered waistcoat and huge flapped coat of the last century who used to parade Broadway. The costume was merely an advertisement, and of very contemptible wares. The man who fights a duel to-day excites but one comment. Should he escape, he is ridiculous. Should he fall, the common opinion of enlightened mankind writes upon his head-stone, "He died as the fool dieth."

(*September*, 1883)

NEWSPAPER ETHICS

I

Newspaper manners and morals hardly fall into the category of minor manners and morals, which are supposed to be the especial care of the Easy Chair, but there are frequent texts upon which the preacher might dilate, and push a discourse upon the subject even to the fifteenthly. Indeed, in this hot time of an opening election campaign, the stress of the contest is so severe that the first condition of a good newspaper is sometimes frightfully maltreated. The first duty of a newspaper is to tell the news; to tell it fairly, honestly, and accurately, which are here only differing aspects of the same adverb. "Cooking the news" is the worst use to which cooking and news can be put. The old divine spoke truly, if with exceeding care, in saying, "It has been sometimes observed that men will lie." So it has been sometimes suspected that newspapers will cook the news.

A courteous interviewer called upon a gentleman to obtain his opinions, let us say, upon the smelt fishery. After the usual civilities upon such occasions, the interviewer remarked, with conscious pride: "The paper that I represent and you, sir, do not agree upon the great smelt question. But it is a newspaper. It prints the facts. It does not pervert them for its own purpose, and it finds its account in it. You may be sure that whatever you may say will be reproduced exactly as you say it. This is the news department. Meanwhile the editorial department will make such comments upon the news as it chooses." This was fair, and the interviewer kept his word. The opinions might be editorially ridiculed from the other smelt point of view, and they probably were so. But the reader of the paper could judge between the opinion and the comment.

Now an interview is no more news than much else that is printed in a paper, and it is no more pardonable to misrepresent other facts than to distort the opinions of the victim of an interview. Yet it has been possible at times to read in the newspapers of the same day accounts of the same proceedings of—of—let us say, as this is election time—of a political convention. The *Banner* informs us that the spirit was unmistakable, and the opinion most decided in favor of Jones. True, the convention voted, by nine hundred to four, for Smith, but there is no doubt that Jones is the name written on the popular heart. The *Standard,* on the other hand, proclaims that the popular heart is engraved all over with the inspiring name of Smith, and that it is impossible to find any trace of feeling for Jones, except, possibly, in the case of one delegate, who is probably an idiot or a lunatic. This is gravely served up as news, and the papers pay for it. They even hire men to write this, and pay them for it. How Ude and Carême would have disdained this kind of cookery! It is questionable whether hanging is not a better use to put a man to than cooking news. Sir Henry Wotton defined an ambassador as an honest man sent to lie abroad for the commonwealth. This kind of purveyor, however, does not lie for his country, but for a party or a person.

It is done with a purpose, the purpose of influencing other action. It is intended to swell the paean for Jones or for Smith, and to procure results under false pretences. Procuring goods under false pretences is a crime, but everybody is supposed to read the newspapers at his own risk. Has the reader yet to learn that newspapers are very human? A paper, for instance, takes a position upon the Jones or Smith question. It decides, upon all the information it can obtain, and by its own deliberate judgment, that Jones is the coming man, or ("it has been observed that men will sometimes lie") it has illicit reasons for the success of Smith. Having thus taken its course, it cooks all the news upon the Smith and Jones controversy, in order that by encouraging the Jonesites or the Smithians, according to the color that it wears, it may promote the success of the side upon which its opinion has been staked. It is a ludicrous and desperate game, but it is certainly not the honest collection and diffusion of news. It is a losing game also, because, whatever the sympathies of the reader, he does not care to be foolishly deceived about the situation. If he is told day after day that Smith is immensely ahead and has a clear field, he is terribly shaken by the shock of learning at the final moment that he has been cheated from the beginning, and that poor Smith is dead upon the field of dishonor.

Everybody is willing to undertake everybody else's business, and an Easy Chair naturally supposes, therefore, that it could show the able editor a plan of securing and retaining a large audience. The plan would be that described by the urbane reporter as the plan of his own paper. It is nothing else than truth-telling in the news column, and the peremptory punishment of all criminals who cook the news, and "write up" the situation, not as it is, but as the paper wishes it to be. This is more than an affair of the private wishes or preferences of the paper. To cook the news is a public wrong, and a violation of the moral contract which the newspaper makes with the public to supply the news, and to use every reasonable effort to obtain it, not to manufacture it, either in the office or by correspondence.

(*July,* 1880)

II

If, as a New York paper recently said, the journalist is superseding the orator, it is full time for the work upon *Journals and Journalism*, which has been lately issued in London. The New York writer holds that in our political contests the "campaign speech" is not intended or adapted to persuade or convert opponents, but merely to stimulate and encourage friends. The party meetings on each side, he thinks, are composed of partisans, and the more extravagant the assertion and the more unsparing the denunciation of "the enemy," the more rapturous the enthusiasm of the audience. In fact, his theory of campaign speeches is that they are merely the addresses of generals to their armies on the eve of battle, which are not arguments, since argument is not needed, but mere urgent appeals to party feeling. "Thirty centuries look down from yonder Pyramid" is the Napoleonic tone of the campaign speech.

As an election is an appeal to the final tribunal of the popular judgment, the apparent object of election oratory is to affect the popular decision. But this, the journalist asserts, is not done by the orator, for the reason just stated, but by the journal. The newspaper addresses the voter, not with rhetorical periods and vapid declamation, but with facts and figures and arguments which the voter can verify and ponder at his leisure, and not under the excitement or the tedium of a spoken harangue. The newspaper, also, unless it be a mere party "organ," is candid to the other side, and states the situation fairly. Moreover, the exigencies of a daily issue and of great space to fill produce a fulness and variety of information and of argument which are really the source of most of the speeches, so that the orator repeats to his audience an imperfect abstract of a complete and ample plea, and the orator, it is asserted, would often serve his cause infinitely better by reading a carefully written newspaper article than by pouring out his loose and illogical declamation.

But the argument for the newspaper can be pushed still further. Since phonographic reporting has become universal, and the speaker is conscious that his very words will be spread the next morning before hundreds of thousands of readers, it is of those readers, and not of the thousand hearers before him, of whom he thinks, and for whom his address is really prepared. Formerly a single charge was all that was needed for the fusillade of a whole political campaign. The speech that was originally carefully prepared was known practically only to the audience that heard it. It grew better and brighter with the attrition of repeated delivery, and was fresh and new to every new audience. But now, when delivered to an audience, it is spoken to the whole country. It is often in type before it is uttered, so that the orator is in fact repeating the article of to-morrow morning. The result is good so far as it compels him to precision of statement, but it inevitably suggests the question whether the newspaper is not correct in its assertion that the great object of the oration is accomplished not by the orator, but by the writer.

But this, after all, is like asking whether a chromo copy of a great picture does not supersede painting, and prove it to be an antiquated or obsolete art. Oratory is an art, and its peculiar charm and power cannot be superseded by any other art. Great orations are now prepared with care, and may be printed word for word. But the reading cannot produce the impression of the hearing. We can all read the words that Webster spoke on Bunker Hill at the laying of the corner-stone of the monument fifty years after the battle. But those who saw him standing there, in his majestic prime, and speaking to that vast throng, heard and saw and felt something that we cannot know. The ordinary stump speech which imperfectly echoes a leading article can well be spared. But the speech of an orator still remains a work of art, the words of which may be accurately lithographed, while the spirit and glow and inspiration of utterance which made it a work of art cannot be reproduced.

The general statement of the critic, however, remains true, and the effective work of a political campaign is certainly done by the newspaper. The newspaper is of two kinds, again—that which shows exclusively the virtue and advantage of the party it favors, and that which aims to be judicial and impartial. The tendency of the first kind is obvious enough, but that of the last is not less positive if less obvious. The tendency of the independent newspaper is to good-natured indifference. The very ardor, often intemperate and indiscreet, with which a side is advocated, prejudices such a paper against the cause itself. Because the hot orator exclaims that the success of the adversary would ruin the country, the independent Mentor gayly suggests that the country is not so easily ruined, and that such an argument is a reason for voting against the orator. The position that in a party contest it is six on one side and half a dozen on the other is too much akin to the doctrine that naught is everything and everything is naught to be very persuasive with men who are really in earnest. Such a position in public affairs inevitably, and often very unjustly to them, produces an impression of want of hearty conviction, which paralyzes influence as effectually as the evident prejudice and partiality of the party advocate. Thorough independence is perfectly compatible with the strongest conviction that the public welfare will be best promoted by the success of this or that party. Such independence criticises its own party and partisans, but it would not have wavered in the support of the Revolution because Gates and Conway were intriguers, and Charles Lee an adventurer, and it would have sustained Sir Robert Walpole although he would not repeal the Corporation and Test laws, and withdrew his excise act.

Journalism, if it be true that it really shapes the policy of nations, well deserves to be treated as thoughtfully as Mr. "John Oldcastle" apparently treats it in the book we have mentioned, for it is the most exacting of professions in the ready use of various knowledge. Mr. Anthony Trollope says that anybody can set up the business or profession of literature who can command a room, a table, and pen, ink, and paper. Would he also say that any man may set up the trade of an artist who can buy an easel, a palette, a few brushes, and some colors? It can be done, indeed, but only as a man who can hire a boat may set up for an East India merchant.

(*December*, 1880)

III

"If you find that you have no case," the old lawyer is reported to have said to the young, "abuse the plaintiff's attorney," and Judge Martin Grover, of New York, used to say that it was apparently a great relief to a lawyer who had lost a case to betake himself to the nearest tavern and swear at the court. Abuse, in any event, seems to have been regarded by both of these authorities as a consolation in defeat. It is but carrying the theory a step further to resort to abuse in argument. Timon, who is a club cynic—which is perhaps the most useless specimen of humanity—says that 'pon his honor nothing entertains him more than to see how little argument goes to the discussion of any question, and how immediate is the recourse to blackguardism. "The other day," he said, recently, "I was sitting in the smoking-room, and Blunt and Sharp began to talk about yachts. Sharp thinks that he knows all that can be known of yachts, and Blunt thinks that what he thinks is unqualified truth. Sharp made a strong assertion, and Blunt smiled. It was that lofty smile of amused pity and superiority, which is, I suppose, very exasperating. Sharp was evidently surprised, but he continued, and at another observation Blunt looked at him, and said, simply, 'Ridiculous!' As it seemed to me," said Timon, "the stronger and truer were the remarks of Sharp, the more Blunt's tone changed from contempt to anger, until he came to a torrent of vituperation, under which Sharp retired from the room with dignity.

"I presume," said the cynic, "that Sharp was correct upon every point. But the more correct Sharp was, the more angry Blunt became. It was very entertaining, and it seems to me very much the way of more serious discussion." Timon was certainly right, and those who heard his remarks, and have since then seen him chuckling over the newspapers, are confident it is because he observes in them the same method of carrying on discussion. Much public debate recalls the two barbaric methods of warfare, which consist in making a loud noise and in emitting vile odors. A member of

Congress pours out a flood of denunciatory words in the utmost rhetorical confusion, and seems to suppose that he has dismayed his opponent because he has made a tremendous noise. He is only an overgrown boy, who, like some other boys, imagines that he is very heroic when he shakes his head, and pouts his lip, and clinches his fist, and "calls names" in a shrill and rasping tone. Other members, who ought to know better, pretend to regard his performances as worthy of applause, and metaphorically pat him on the back and cry, "St, boy!" They only share—and in a greater degree, because they know better—the contempt with which he is regarded.

In the same way a newspaper writer attacks views which are not acceptable to him, not with argument, or satire, or wit, or direct refutation, but by metaphorically emptying slops, and directing whirlwinds of bad smells upon their supporters. The intention seems to be, not to confute the arguments, but to disgust the advocates. The proceeding is a confession that the views are so evidently correct that they will inevitably prevail unless their supporters can be driven away. This is an ingenious policy, for guns certainly cannot be served if the gunners are dispersed. Men shrink from ridicule and ludicrous publicity. However conscious of rectitude a man may be, it is exceedingly disagreeable for him to see the dead-walls and pavements covered with posters proclaiming that he is a liar and a fool. If he recoils, the enemy laughs in triumph; if he is indifferent, there is a fresh whirlwind.

A public man wrote recently to a friend that he had seen an attack upon his conduct in a great journal, and had asked his lawyer to take the necessary legal steps to bring the offender to justice. His friend replied that he had seen the attack, but that it had no more effect upon him than the smells from Newtown Creek. They were very disgusting, but that was all. This is the inevitable result of blackguardism. The newspaper reader, as he sees that one man supports one measure because his wife's uncle is interested in it, and another man another measure to gratify his grudge against a rival, gradually learns from his daily morning mentor that there is no such thing as honor, decency, or public spirit in public affairs; he chuckles with the club cynic, although for a very different reason, and forgets the contents of one column as he begins upon the next. If a man covers his milk toast, his breakfast, his lunch, dinner, and supper with a coating of Cayenne pepper, the pepper becomes as things in general became to Mr. Toots—of no consequence.

This kind of fury in personal denunciation is not force, as young writers suppose; it is feebleness. Wit, satire, brilliant sarcasm, are, indeed, legitimate weapons. It was these which Sydney Smith wielded in the early *Edinburgh Review*. But "calling names," and echoing the commonplaces of affected contempt, that is too weak even for Timon to chuckle over, except as evidence of mental vacuity. The real object in honest controversy is to defeat your opponent and leave him a friend. But the Newtown Creek method is fatal to such a result. Of course that method often apparently wins. But it always fails when directed against a resolute and earnest purpose. The great causes persist through seeming defeat to victory. But to oppose them with sneers and blackguardism is to affect to dam Niagara with a piece of paper. The crafty old lawyer advised the younger to reserve his abuse until he felt that he had no case. Judge Grover remarked that it was when the case was lost that the profanity began.

(*September*, 1882)

IV

There is a delicate question in newspaper ethics which is sometimes widely discussed, namely, whether "journalism" may be regarded as a distinct profession which has a moral standard of its own. The question arises when an editorial writer transfers his services from one journal to another of different political opinions. Is a man justified in arguing strenuously for free trade to-day and for protection to-morrow? Are political questions and measures of public policy merely points of law upon which an editor is an advocate to be retained indifferently and with equal morality upon either side?

This question may be illuminated by another. Would John Bright be a man of equal renown, character, and weight of influence if, being an adherent of peace principles, he had remained in an administration whose policy was war? This question will be thought to beg the whole question. But does it? Must it not be assumed that a man of adequate ability for the proper discussion of political questions must have positive political convictions, and can a man who has such convictions honorably devote himself to discrediting them, and to defeating the policy which they demand, under the plea that he has professionally accepted a retainer or a salary to do so? Would his arguments have any moral weight if they were known to be those of a man who was not himself convinced by them? And is not the concealment of the fact indispensable to the value of his services?

To continue this interrogation: is not the parallel sought to be established between the editorial writer and the lawyer vitiated by the fact that it is universally understood that a lawyer's service is perfunctory and official; that he takes one side rather than another because he is paid for it, and because that is the condition of his profession, and that that condition springs from the nature of legal procedure, society not choosing to take life or to inflict punishment of any kind until the whole case has been stated according to certain stipulated forms? For this reason the advocate who defends a criminal is not supposed necessarily to believe him to be innocent. But no such reason existing in the case of the editor, is it not an equally universal understanding that an editor does honestly and personally hold the view that he presents and defends? For instance, the *Times* in New York is a Republican and free-trade journal. If it should suddenly appear some morning as a Democratic and protectionist paper, would not the general conclusion be that it had changed hands? But if it should be announced that it was in the same hands, and had changed its views because of a pecuniary arrangement, could the *Times* continue to have the same standing and influence which it has now?

A distinction may be attempted between the owner of a paper and the editor. But for the public are they not practically the same? It is not, in fact, the owner or the editor, it is the paper, which is known to the public. If the public considers at all the probable relation of the owner and editor, it necessarily assumes their harmony, because it does not suppose that an owner would employ an editor who is injuring the property, and if the paper flourishes under the editor, it is because the owner yields his private opinion to the editor's, if they happen to differ, so that there is no discord. On the other hand, if the paper flags and fails, and the owner, to rescue his property, employs another editor, who holds other views, and changes the tone of the paper, the result is the same so far as the public is concerned. The profit of the paper may increase, but its power and influence surely decline. In the illustration that we have supposed, the proprietorship of the *Times* might decide that a Democratic and protection paper would have a larger sale and greatly increase the profit. But could the change be made without a terrible blow to the character and influence of the paper? Now why is not an editor in the same position? He has a certain standing, and he holds certain views, like the paper. The paper changes its tone for a price. He does the same thing. The paper loses character and influence. Why does not he?

Journalism is not a profession in the sense claimed. It does not demand a certain course of study, which is finally tested by an examination and certified by a degree. It is a pursuit rather than a profession. Of course special knowledge in particular branches of information is of the highest value, and indeed essential to satisfactory editorial writing, as to all other public exposition. There are also certain details of the collection of news, the organization of correspondence, and the "make up" of the paper, the successful management of which depends upon an energetic executive faculty, which is desirable in every pursuit. It is sometimes said that an editor, like the late Mr. Delane of the London *Times*, should not write himself, but select the topics and procure the writing upon them by others. And so long as a man is merely an anonymous writer for a paper, so long as he writes to sustain the views of the paper, his actual opinions, being unknown to the reader, do not affect the power of the paper. Such a man, indeed, may write at the same time upon both sides of the same question for different papers. But if he have any convictions or opinions upon the subject, he is with one hand consciously injuring what he believes to be the truth, and a man cannot do that without serious harm to himself. If he have no convictions, his influence will vanish the moment that the fact is known.

Such strictures do not apply to papers which expressly renounce convictions, and blow hot or cold as the chances of probable profit and the apparent tenor of public opinion at the moment invite. Such papers, properly speaking, have no legitimate influence whatever. They produce a certain effect by mere publicity, and reiteration, and ridicule, and distortion and suppression of facts, and appeals to prejudice. There is a legitimate and an illegitimate power of the press. A lion and a skunk both inspire terror.

But a paper which represents convictions, and promotes a public policy in accordance with them, necessarily implies sincerity in its editorial writing. The public assumes that among papers of all opinions the writer attaches himself to one with which he agrees. The nature of the pursuit is such that he cannot make himself a free lance without running the risk of being thought an adventurer, a soldier without patriotism, a citizen without convictions. If the best American press did not represent real convictions, but only the clever ingenuity of paid advocates, it would be worthless as an exponent of public opinion, and could not be the beneficent power that it is.

(*October*, 1882)

V

One public man in a recent angry altercation with another taunted him with elaborately preparing his invective, and some notoriously vituperative speeches are known to have been written out and printed before they were spoken. Such cold venom is undoubtedly as effective in reading as the hot outbreak of the moment, and it may be even more effective in the delivery, since self-command is as useful to the orator as to the actor. But if a man be guilty of a gross offence who upon a dignified scene violates the self-restraint and respect for the company which are not only becoming, but so much assumed that whoever violates the requirement is felt to insult his associates and the public, why do we not consider whether every scene is not too dignified for mature and intelligent men to attempt to rival in blackguardism the traditional fishwives of Billingsgate?

If an orator or a newspaper conducts a discussion without discharging the fiercest and foulest epithets at the opponent, it is often declared to be tame and feeble and indifferent. But to whom and to what does vituperation appeal? When an advocate upon the platform shouts until he is very hot and very red that the supporter of protection is a thief, a robber, a pampered pet of an atrociously diabolical system, he inflames passion and prejudice, indeed, to the highest fury, and he produces a state of mind which is inaccessible to reason, but he does not show in any degree whatever either that protection is inexpedient or how it is unjust. In the same way, to assail an opponent who favors revision of the tariff and incidental protection as a rascally scoundrel who is trying to ruin American industry—as if he could have any purpose of injuring himself materially and fatally—is absurd. The tirade merely injures the cause which the blackguard intends to help. But the man who carried on discussion in this style is described by other professors of the same art as manly and virile and hitting from the shoulder, and he comes perhaps to think himself a doughty champion of the right.

The weapon that demolishes an antagonist and an argument is not rhetoric, but truth. This accumulation of "bad names" and ingenious combination of scurrility is merely rhetoric. It serves the rhetorical purpose, but it does not convince. It does not show the hearer or reader that one course is more expedient than another, nor give him any reason whatever for any opinion upon the subject. Virility, vigor, masculinity of mind, and essential force in debate are revealed in quite another way. If an American were asked to mention the most powerful speech ever made in the debates of Congress, he would probably mention Mr. Webster's reply to Hayne. It contained the great statement of nationality and the argument for the national interpretation of the Constitution, and it was spoken in the course of a famous controversy. Let any man read it, and ask himself whether it would have gained in power, in effect, in weight, dignity, or character, by personal invective and elaborate vituperation of any kind and any degree whatever.

The truth is that the fury which is supposed to imply force is the conclusive proof of weakness. The familiar advice, "If you have no evidence, abuse the plaintiff's attorney," contains by implication the whole philosophy of what is called the manliness and force of the blackguard. He has no reason, therefore he sneers. He has no argument, therefore he swears. He will get the laugh upon his adversary if he can, forgetting that those who laugh at the clown may also despise him.

Of wit, humor, satire, sarcasm, we are not speaking. The ordinary blackguardism of the political platform and press does not belong to that category. Caricature, however, easily may. There are certain pictures in

American caricature which are wit made visible. They are the satire of instructive truth. Indeed, they tell to the eye the indisputable truth as words cannot easily tell it to the ear. In this way caricature is one of the most powerful agents in public discussion. But, like speech or writing, it may be merely blackguard. The incisive wit, the rich humor, the withering satire of speech, gain all their point and effect from the truth. They have no power when they are seen to be false.

So it is with caricature. Nobody can enjoy it more than its subject when it is merely humorous; nobody perceive so surely its pungent touch of truth; nobody disregard more completely its mere malice and falsehood. True wit and humor, whether in controversial letters or art, whether in the newspaper article or the "cartoon," as we now call it, often reveal to the subject in himself what otherwise he might not have suspected. It is very conceivable that an actor, seeing a really clever burlesque of himself, may become aware of tendencies or peculiarities or faults which otherwise he would not have known, and quietly address himself to their correction.

This sanitary service of humor in every form, as well as that of the honest wrath which shakes many a noble sentence of sinewy English as a mighty man-of-war is shaken by her own broadside, is something wholly apart from the billingsgate and blackguardism which are treated as if they were real forces. Publicity itself, as the Easy Chair has often said, has a certain power, and to call a man a rascal to a hundred thousand persons at once produces an undeniable effect. But we must not mistake it for what it is not. Being false, it is not an effect which endures, nor does it vex the equal mind.

It is the fact that the public often seems to demand that kind of titillation, to enjoy fury instead of force, and ridicule instead of reason, which suggests the inquiry whether, if self-restraint and wise discipline are desirable for every faculty of the mind and body, the tongue and hand alone should be allowed to riot in wanton excess. If even the legitimate superlative must be handled, like dynamite, with extreme caution, blackguardism of every degree is a nuisance to be summarily discountenanced and abated by those who know the difference between grandeur and bigness, between Mercutio and Tony Lumpkin, between fair-play and foul.

(*September*, 1888)

VI

The Easy Chair has been asked whether there is any code of newspaper manners. It has no doubt that there is. But it is the universal code of courtesy, and not one restricted to newspapers. Good manners in civilized society are the same everywhere and in all relations. A newspaper is not a mystery. It is the work of several men and women, and their manners in doing the work are subject to the same principles that govern their manners in society or in any other human relation. If a man is a gentleman, he does not cease to be one because he enters a newspaper office, and it would seem to be equally true that if his work on the paper does not prove to be that of a gentleman, it could not have been a gentleman who did the work.

A gentleman, we will suppose, does not blackguard his neighbors, nor talk incessantly about himself and his achievements, nor behave elsewhere as he would be ashamed to behave in his club or in his own family. If a gentleman does not do these things, of course a gentleman does not do them in a newspaper. And does it not seem to follow, if such things are done in a newspaper, and are traced to a hand supposed to be that of a gentleman, that there has been some mistake about the hand?

Good manners are essentially a disposition which moulds conduct. They can be feigned, indeed, as gilt counterfeits gold, and plate silver. But the clearest glass is not diamond. A man may smile and smile and be a villain. Scoundrels are sometimes described as of gentlemanly manners, and Lothario was not personally a boor. But he was not a gentleman, and he merely affected good manners. A gentleman, indeed, may sometimes lose his temper or his self-control, but no one who habitually does it, and swears and rails vociferously, can be called properly by that name. Here again it is easy to apply the canon to a newspaper. When a newspaper habitually takes an insulting tone, and deliberately falsifies, whether by assertion of an untruth or by a distortion and perversion of the truth, it is not the work of a gentleman, and if the writer be responsible for the tone of the paper, the manners of that newspaper are not good manners.

But there is no uniformity in newspaper manners, as there is none elsewhere. Therefore it cannot be said that newspapers, as a whole, are either well-mannered or unmannerly, as you cannot say that men, as a body, are courteous or uncouth. Some newspapers are unmistakably vulgar, like some people. They are not so of themselves, however; they are made vulgar by vulgar people. There are very able newspapers which have very bad manners, and some which have no other distinction than good manners. A very dull man may be very urbane, and so may a very dull newspaper. On the other hand, a newspaper which is both brilliant and clever may be sometimes guilty of an injustice, a deliberate and persistent misrepresentation, to attain a particular end—conduct which is sometimes called "journalistic." But the person who is responsible for the performance, for similar conduct would be metaphorically kicked out of a club. But gentlemen are not kicked out of clubs.

A newspaper gains neither character nor influence by abandoning good manners. It may indeed make itself disagreeable and annoying, and so silence opposition, as a polecat may effectually close the wood path which you had designed to take. It may be feared, and in the same way as that animal—feared and despised. But this effect must not be confounded with newspaper power and influence. It is exceedingly annoying, undoubtedly, to be placarded all over town as a liar or a donkey, a hypocrite or a sneak-thief. But although the effect is most unpleasant, very little ability is required to produce it. A little paper and printing, a little paste, a great deal of malice, and a host of bill-stickers are all that are needed, and even the pecuniary cost is not large. The effect is produced, but it does not show ability or force or influence upon the part of its producer.

The manners of newspapers, as such, cannot be classified any more than the manners of legislatures, or of the professions or trades. This, however, seems to be true, that a well-mannered man will not produce an ill-mannered newspaper.

(*April*, 1891)